Geronimo

A Captivating Guide to One of the Most Well-Known Native Americans Who Was a Leader of the Apache Tribe and a Prominent Figure of the Wild West

Free Bonus from Captivating History (Available for a Limited time)

Hi History Lovers!

Now you have a chance to join our exclusive history list so you can get your first history ebook for free as well as discounts and a potential to get more history books for free! Simply visit the link below to join.

Captivatinghistory.com/ebook

Also, make sure to follow us on Facebook, Twitter and Youtube by searching for Captivating History.

Contents

Introduction

His name was Geronimo. And any mention of that name immediately conjures up images of the last gasp of Native American control of the Western Frontier. Geronimo, to be sure, was one of the most effective leaders in the resistance against America's westward advance, but he was much more than just a good field commander for the Apaches.

For even after the West was supposedly won, Geronimo proved more than ready to adapt. And when the Apache Wars came to a close, he was able to rebrand himself as an icon of Western Americana. In many instances, he actually got paid by the very ones who thought they had vanquished him, as Geronimo became a kind of celebrity, participating in Wild West shows in which he basically acted out what was his life—or at least what was perceived to be his life. But in reality, the real Geronimo was much more than an accomplished horseman riding the range. He was more than a marauder raiding hapless settlers. And he was more than a skilled marksman, medicine man, and shaman.

Geronimo was far more than the Wild West caricature that he was later made out to be; he was a real flesh and blood man who had real emotions, real hopes, and real dreams. He had a wife—actually wives—of his own, and he had children whom he dearly loved. For most, "family man" probably doesn't come to mind when gazing at the old black and white photos of Geronimo's grim visage, but he was a deeply dedicated husband and father.

As harsh and cruel as he was known to be on the battlefield, he could be just as kind and gentle when he was away from it. In this text, you will get the full picture of Geronimo: the good, the bad, and the downright incredible.

Chapter 1 – The Days of His Youth

Although his birth year is not known for certain, it is believed to have been around 1829. He was a part of the Bedonkohe band of the Chiricahua tribe, which was a part of the larger Apache group, and his grandfather had been a chief. Growing up, Geronimo lived a relatively carefree life as a child, playing and roaming about his ancestral lands. As he neared adolescence, however, it became incumbent upon him to prove his worth as a man. For it was at this time that he entered into what was known as his "novice" period.

This was the point in time in which it was ingrained upon a young man from the Apache tribe to prove that they could hold their own. This meant learning how to hunt, fight, and ride a horse just like any other member of the tribe. It was during the course of this quest for manhood that Geronimo's father, Taslishim, introduced him to a tribal elder who instructed him how to build his own "sacred bow and arrows."

This was a rite of passage that enabled Geronimo to begin life as a full-fledged member of the tribe who could hunt wild game on his own. Along with hunting, he was also shown how to adapt to the harsh environment of the Apache homeland, which at that time stretched across the desert sands of the southwestern United States. These lessons included endurance training, in which Geronimo would learn to survive without water and even improve his breathing.

To improve his breathing, he would be sent on long runs across the desert terrain during which he would purposefully keep his mouth closed so that he would be forced to inhale and exhale nasally, rather than orally. This was a technique that had been refined by the Apache for generations in order to teach adherents how to build up their lung capacity. In order to perfect the method, Geronimo himself would later recall how he would bite down on rocks he had placed in his mouth so that he was left with no choice but to inhale through his nasal passages.

Geronimo is thought to have been around ten years old when he was engrossed in these rigorous exercises, and by Apache standards, he was very successful in his efforts to transition from a young boy to a man. However, Geronimo wouldn't have long to celebrate this rite of passage before the abrupt death of his father, Taslishim.

With the death of his father, young Geronimo was officially considered the head of his household. Nevertheless, he still had to complete his training. With his father out of the picture, this important form of mentorship most likely fell upon the able shoulders of an uncle or a similar relative.

Under this tutelage, Geronimo further perfected his hunting skills, as well as his ability to ride a horse. Buffalo, deer, and pronghorn antelope were some of the real prizes during these forays out on the range, but turkeys and rabbits were acceptable fare as well. The hunt for turkeys, in particular, was a real sight to behold. It involved a band of Apache flushing out the birds and then relentlessly chasing them until the animals simply became too exhausted and gave up.

In the years after his father's passing, Geronimo became quite skilled at hunting all manner of wildlife. But the final trial that Geronimo needed to pass was not one that involved animals; instead, it involved people. The capstone experience of his Apache training would not rest on how well he hunted turkey and buffalo but rather how well he would perform in raiding settlements.

Although the Apache were skilled hunters and knew how to live off the land, a mainstay of their existence involved the launching of raiding parties against their rivals. Geronimo was seventeen years old when he went on his first raid. A special shaman accompanied Geronimo and the other initiates for their first raid and served as counsel during the course of the exercise.

Beforehand, he gave the young men special ceremonial clothing to wear, such as a special jacket and hat that were said to "protect men in battle." Along with this protective gear, the shaman also gave them prudent advice as to what they should expect during the raid. This was a make-or-break moment for Geronimo and his peers because if they proved to be ineffective during the raid, or, even worse, if they displayed cowardice, they would have the stigma of their failure follow them for the rest of their lives.

Those that displayed true courage and cunning, however, would be welcomed in as a full-fledged member of the tribe. Knowing the stakes, Geronimo carefully prepared for his first raid, making sure to follow every piece of advice that the shaman gave. Fortunately for Geronimo, he passed his test with flying colors. He was considered to have performed admirably during the course of the raid and therefore was made a full-fledged member of the tribe.

Geronimo would later recall just how proud he felt on this occasion. He would reflect, "I was very happy, for I could go wherever I wanted and do whatever I liked." As a full-fledged member of the tribe, Geronimo had the freedom to be his own man. He was a free agent on the Apache range, and very soon, he would become a free agent of his own destiny.

Chapter 2 – Geronimo Comes into His Own

With his ascendency as a full member of the tribe assured, Geronimo was now able to take his official place as an Apache. This meant that he would marry and start a family of his own. The woman he chose hailed from the Nednhi tribe, and she was known by the name of Alope. Not much else is known about Alope, but she must have been greatly loved by her family since Geronimo paid them a large dowry in the form of numerous horses. These animals were most likely stolen from ranches in northern Mexico during subsequent Apache raids launched in the area.

After paying this dowry, Geronimo took Alope to be his wife. There was no wedding ceremony; instead, he simply set up his semi-nomadic dwelling, known as a wickiup, and invited Alope inside. This mobile home on the range already held all of Geronimo's hunting gear, such as knives, spears, and arrows. Alope did her best to spruce up their new place by adding beaded decorations and "wall paintings."

Geronimo was fond of his wife but always kept any mention of her fairly brief. He would later recall, "She was a good wife, but she was never strong. We followed the traditions of our fathers and were happy. Three children came to us—children that played, loitered, and worked as I had done." By this time, Geronimo was the head of a growing family, and his own personal renown was growing as well.

Geronimo had become an acknowledged veteran in the field, and in the dangerous world in which he lived, all of his finely honed skills would be necessary for the survival of himself, his family, and his tribe. By the time he was in his early twenties, Geronimo had taken part in several armed conflicts, primarily in Mexico. In the fall of 1846, in particular, Geronimo took part in a massive conflict with Mexican forces that involved around 175 Apaches.

The year 1846 was a pivotal one, as a war broke out between the United States and Mexico that very year due to a disagreement over the Mexico/Texas border. The war would end in 1848, with the Americans victorious and Mexico defeated. As a result of the American victory, Mexico was forced to sign the Treaty of Guadalupe Hidalgo, which ceded much of what today comprises the American Southwest to the United States.

After the end of the Mexican-American War, an exhausted Mexico, weary of fighting, developed a policy of appeasement when it came to the Apache by installing "feeding stations" at the edge of Apache territory. These were designated areas where food and supplies were left for the Apaches to pick up of their own accord. This was done in order to prevent them from conducting further raids in Mexican territory.

As long as they gave the Apache these handouts, it kept them from going on the warpath to take things by force. And for a while, the situation remained one of relative peace, and an official peace agreement between local Apache and Mexican authorities was entered into on June 24th, 1850. But a short time later, the Mexicans began to withdraw the feeding stations, and soon after, the Apache raids resumed.

This resurgent conflict would touch Geronimo far closer to home than he could have ever imagined, for it was in 1851 that disaster would strike. Geronimo and a small band of Apache warriors had left their wives and children camped out on the outskirts of Mexico while they went into a nearby town to trade. While he was gone, a Mexican militia stumbled upon Geronimo's camp and slaughtered the inhabitants.

A distraught Geronimo returned to find that his wife, his children, and even his mother had all been killed. Along with their deaths, he found that all of his supplies, arms, and food had been confiscated as well. This was certainly a black day for Geronimo, and he would remember it for the rest of his life. As Geronimo himself would later recall, "I had lost all. I was never again contented in our quiet home. True, I could visit my father's grave, but I had vowed vengeance upon the Mexican troopers who had wronged me, and whenever I came near his grave or saw anything to remind me of former happy days my heart would ache for revenge against Mexico."

Geronimo wanted to seek out immediate revenge, but when his comrades advised him that such a move would be futile, as they were outnumbered and in Mexican territory, Geronimo was finally convinced to withdraw. Upon returning to Apache lands, Geronimo attended a council of war and made sure that reprisal against Mexico was a top priority. At this time, Geronimo's chief was a man named Mangas Coloradas.

Mangas Coloradas had managed to unify his tribe with another local chapter by marrying his daughter to a chief named Cochise. It was to Cochise that Mangas sent Geronimo in order to cobble together enough braves from the allied tribes to stage a retaliatory strike. This group of assembled warriors set up camp near the town of Arispe on the Mexican border.

It wasn't long before Mexican officials were informed of the group's arrival. Initially, it wasn't clear what Geronimo and his band were there for. This wasn't the first time the Apache had come to this Mexican town since it was a major hub of commerce in the region. As such, the Mexicans didn't know whether they had come to do battle or to do business. In order to get to the bottom of the situation, the Mexicans sent a small scouting party to inquire as to what the Apaches were up to.

These Apache warriors were not interested in answering questions, however, and instead attacked the approaching Mexicans. This unlucky envoy was overwhelmed, and every last man was killed. It was after the scouting party failed to return that the local garrison realized that they had a real problem on their hands. In order to face the threat that was camped just outside of town, they quickly mobilized a militia that could take on the waiting Apache.

Knowing that the real battle was growing near, the Apache began to feverishly prepare for their main assault on the town. This engagement occurred at around ten o'clock the next morning. As the fighting commenced, there was no doubt who was in charge of the Apaches. Geronimo would later recall, "I was no chief and never had been, but because I had been more deeply wronged than the others, this honor was conferred upon me, and I resolved to prove worthy of the trust."

His warriors were assembled in what Geronimo called a "hollow circle." They remained in this position until the Mexican militia approached. Then, as soon as the Mexican troops were within a few hundred yards, the Apache opened fire on them. Just as the Mexicans began to fire their weapons, the Apache charged, attempting to overwhelm the enemy with their ferocity.

But the opposition was equally fierce, and soon, Apache warriors were falling down left and right. Geronimo himself came dangerously close to being killed at one point when the Mexicans closed in around him. By using the cunning maneuverability tactics he had learned in his many years of training, he was able to evade his attackers.

Upon regaining his footing on more stable ground, Geronimo then turned the tables on his pursuers. At one point, he managed to grab a slain Mexican's sword and used it to hack into a couple of nearby Mexicans. It was the ferocity of Geronimo and his band that ended up winning the day.

It is believed that this conflict occurred sometime around 1851, although the date cannot be known for certain. Whatever the case may be, from that day forward, Geronimo was seen as a leader and a man of distinction.

Chapter 3 – Geronimo Continues His Quest

It was a stunning victory that Geronimo had achieved against the Mexican forces, but he wasn't through yet. After this initial strike against Mexican power in the region, Geronimo took his band of followers even deeper into enemy territory and had them hole up in the Sierra de Antunez Mountains.

It was while they were in the Sierra de Antunez range that Geronimo found a new target on which to launch an assault—a sleepy little Mexican village at the foot of the mountains. Although this band of marauders probably thought that the village was easy pickings, as soon as they stepped out from the mountains, they found a fully armed Mexican militia waiting for them.

A firefight then ensued, with the Mexicans and Apaches becoming embroiled in a bloody and protracted battle, as the Apaches attempted to gain a foothold and the Mexicans struggled to push them out. During the course of the carnage, there were numerous instances in which Geronimo almost lost his life. But in the end, Geronimo escaped unscathed, and realizing that this battle was a lost cause, he managed to lead his men out of the fray and back up the mountains. Although it was the able leadership of Geronimo that allowed for this escape to be possible, many of his men openly accused him of both cowardice and incompetence.

To be sure, the raid was indeed a failure, and to make matters worse, the braves had left their families vulnerable and undefended back at their camp. This was something that the Mexicans had anticipated, and in the continuous cycle of carnage between the Native Americans and Mexicans, civilians were very much fair game when it came to reprisals. Geronimo, realizing the vulnerability of those they had left behind, rushed back to the encampment just in time to fend off a Mexican militia.

When the Mexicans fled, Geronimo and his men were able to pursue them from a distance. The Mexicans eventually led them right to their own base in the mountains. Geronimo, the master strategist, always looking for an opportunity, had his men assemble nearby and prepared to strike. At first, they tried to shoot the Mexicans out of their hideout, but it soon turned into a melee. And it slowly became clear that the Apaches were running out of ammo.

Geronimo, knowing that this battle had to be won—and won quickly—signaled for the braves to descend to take the Mexicans out at close range. Geronimo led the assault, and he almost met his end when he lost his footing in a "pool of blood" and fell down on the ground. Seeing the prone Geronimo, a Mexican rushed over and struck him in the back of his skull with the end of his rifle. Geronimo was nearly knocked out from the blow.

The Mexican was in the process of finishing the Apache commander off when one of Geronimo's fellow braves managed to save the day by charging forward and engaging his attacker. Geronimo was gathered up by other comrades who had been alerted to his plight, and they carried him off the battlefield so that he could recover. Even though Geronimo was taken out of the fight, his men continued the engagement and managed to achieve a total victory against the Mexicans.

Geronimo would have been pleased if he had been awake, but as it were, he was completely out of it at the time, sleeping some distance away. There was no time for a nap, however, and his men quickly brought him back to reality by splashing water in his face. Once he regained consciousness, they bandaged the wounded warrior up, and the whole group headed back to the camp.

It would take a while for Geronimo to heal from the wounds he had received, and with their commander out of commission, his band of loyal Apache would just have to hold their fire. Geronimo would wait it out until 1861 before he once again struck out against the Mexicans. Geronimo's next assault would occur while he and his group traversed through the Sierra Madre range, which runs through northern Mexico. Here, they came upon a convoy that included a bunch of mules, donkeys, and other beasts of burden, which were loaded with food and ammo.

For a band of marauders like Geronimo and his Apache, this was just too much to resist. Perched from on high, Geronimo signaled his men to charge down on the travelers as they made their way through the mountain pass. Taken by surprise, the frightened Mexicans took one look at the Apaches charging at them and took off, leaving all of their supplies behind.

The Apaches were more than happy to let them depart as long as they could grab their belongings. But it seems that what goes around comes around because Geronimo and his Apache were likewise waylaid by a group of Mexicans shortly thereafter. According to Geronimo's own later recollection, "It was at daybreak and we were just finishing our breakfast. We had no idea that we had been pursued or that our enemies were near until they opened fire."

As the Mexicans opened up on the Apaches, Geronimo himself would have a bullet graze across his "left eye," causing him to reel backward and fall to the ground. It was a minor wound, but Geronimo's enemies apparently took him for dead, for as they chased off the rest of the Apache, they left him there lying in his own blood. It took Geronimo a few minutes to recover his senses, but he finally managed to rouse himself and escape into the wilderness.

Some of the Mexican troops saw his mad dash and began to shoot at the fleeing figure of Geronimo. According to his account, he just "kept running, dodging, and fighting" until he managed to get out of range of his assailants. He suffered another minor "flesh wound" in his side during the melee, but he otherwise managed to escape without mortal injury. As was the custom, Geronimo had previously instructed all of his warriors to return to a preordained location in case they became scattered.

And sure enough, a few days later, Geronimo and several others arrived at the Santa Bita Mountains, where they discussed what they should do next. They didn't have long to lick their wounds before their enemies struck them once again. A Mexican militia managed to catch Geronimo and his men off guard, and the Apaches were forced to run for their lives and leave all of their supplies and ammunition behind.

However, that's not all they left behind because, as Geronimo would later recall, "Many women and children and a few warriors were killed, and four women were captured." Geronimo would then relate how he later received word that some of the women taken prisoner were actually taken back to Mexico to be used as forced labor.

This tale has a happy ending, though. According to Geronimo, the women managed to escape those who held them, and they found their way back to the tribe. These women displayed the steely-eyed determination that the Apache were known for. And it was this fighting spirit that Geronimo very much wished to channel in his continued quest for revenge.

Chapter 4 – The Apaches Go on the Warpath

Not a lot is known about how Geronimo spent the next few years of his life, but before the decade was through, he had married two other women—Chee-Hash-Kish and Nana-Tha-Thtith. The Apaches, at this time, practiced polygamy, and as long as a man could support them, he was free to marry as many wives as he wished. It was with Chee-Hash-Kish that Geronimo would have a son named Chappo and a daughter named Dohn-say. Nana-Tha-Thtith, meanwhile, would give Geronimo a third child, whose name was not recorded. Sadly, both Nana-Tha-Thtith and her child would be killed in subsequent engagements with the Mexicans in 1861.

That same year, President Abraham Lincoln would be sworn into office, and the United States found itself in absolute turmoil. Due to tensions over slavery between the free North and slave-holding South, by the time Lincoln began his term, several states had already left the Union. Geronimo and his fellow Apaches in the American Southwest were fairly far removed from the fray, but as the war began to heat up, even they would be affected.

It was only a short time before volunteers began to travel from California, passing through Apache lands to join the Union fight against the Confederate strongholds in the Southeast. The war also impacted traditional routes that led west, which had previously circumvented Apache territory. Unable to go around Apache lands because of the fighting between the Union and the Confederacy, those wishing to head out west were forced to push right through Apache territory.

All of these things combined would inevitably lead to confrontation and conflict, as the newcomers stumbled right into the Apache. It was along the aptly named "Apache Pass" that most of these confrontations would take place. Apache Pass is situated inside a mountainous region of Arizona. At the time, the Apache steward of this region was the powerful chief with whom Geronimo himself had direct dealings, a man named Cochise.

Chief Cochise had entered into various agreements with the United States in the past in regards to traffic through Apache territory. In 1858, in fact, he had crafted an agreement in which he granted safe passage to the US Postal Service and other shipping companies when they had to deliver letters and packages to California. But once the Civil War began in 1861, the situation had become incredibly tense.

The first major conflict between the Americans and the Apaches erupted in the spring of 1861 when the stepson of a local American man by the name of John Ward was abducted by the Apache. Ward aired his grievances to the nearby military installation of Fort Buchanan. The burden of recovering the child then fell onto the shoulders of Second Lieutenant George Nicholas Bascom.

Bascom left the base with a search party comprised of 54 troops to scour Apache Pass for any sign of the boy. They set up camp in the region right as Chief Cochise happened onto the scene. It must be noted that Cochise knew nothing of the kidnapping at the time and that he had no reason to believe that his previously good relations with the US Army had soured.

As such, when he was called over to pay a visit to Lieutenant Bascom's tent, he thought nothing of it. But he was quickly double-crossed. As soon as he stepped into the tent, he was told he would be held hostage until the kidnapped child was returned. Cochise, not willing to be made into anyone's pawn, had an ace—or in his case a knife—up his sleeve, and he was able to slice his way out of the tent.

Running on pure adrenaline, Cochise fled through the hole he had torn through the tent's fabric and took off as fast as his feet could carry him. But unfortunately for Cochise, he was not alone that day; his wife and children had been in attendance with him as well. And although Cochise managed to escape, they could not. His family members would become bargaining chips for the US Army, and they were held as hostages for further negotiations with the Apache.

Despite the duplicitousness with which he had been dealt, Cochise, who was just as good of a peacemaker as he was at making war, attempted to broker an agreement with the Americans the following day. He arrived near the camp with a small entourage of Apache and raised the white flag as a sign that he wished to enter into negotiations with them. Some American troops and an interpreter came out and entered into dialogue with Cochise.

In the discussion, Concise insisted that he was not involved with the missing child's disappearance. But the Americans didn't want to hear it, and they made it clear that the chief's family members would not be returned until he had located the child and brought him back. In the midst of this turmoil, a representative from the US side of the discussion later decided to head over to Cochise's camp to see if he could negotiate matters directly with the chief himself. This proved to be a bad move because as soon as he arrived, the Apaches seized him and made him a hostage. In this cycle of never-ending drama, this man was then held for the ransom of Cochise's own family, which were, in turn, being held for the return of the missing boy.

The very next day, Geronimo, fresh from the warpath in Mexico, arrived on this troubling scene. However, it was about to get even more troubling because Cochise, seeking to gain even more leverage with the Americans, decided that he was going to obtain more hostages to negotiate with. It was in these efforts that he had

Geronimo and several Apache lay in wait for unwary travelers that they could waylay along Apache Pass.

It was in this manner that they took a group of people from a wagon train that had the misfortune of passing through. With his new hostages secure, Cochise went back to the US military encampment and demanded a trade of his hostages for his family. But it was a no-go. Bascom was only interested in retrieving the missing boy and steadfastly refused to take part in any further negotiations until the child was produced.

Frustrated, on February 8th, 1861, Cochise directed Geronimo and his men to attempt another kidnapping at Apache Pass, but this new group of travelers, who had been apparently alerted to the danger they faced, put up a ferocious fight. During the ensuing battle, American troops arrived on the scene. The Apaches were not prepared for this stiff resistance and had to make a hasty retreat.

Before leaving, however, they killed their remaining hostages, leaving their discarded corpses behind. In response to this outrage, the American troops summarily executed two of Cochise's nephews and his brother, who had been under their care. It was now clear that the negotiations were over and that an all-out war between the Apache and the American forces stationed in the area was about to begin.

Chapter 5 – The Greatest Wrong

The early 1860s proved to be a pivotal time for the Apache in general and Geronimo in particular. While Chief Cochise was caught up in continued conflicts and intrigue with the US Army, Geronimo was on the warpath in Chihuahua, located in northern Mexico. It was during one of these exchanges that Geronimo sustained some pretty serious injuries. He had just barely recovered from his wounds when he was forced to flee from Mexico to Arizona.

Mexican militias were in hot pursuit of Geronimo and his men, though, and they sought to wreak vengeance upon Geronimo's camp. The day of reckoning came when the militia observed the main group of warriors leaving the encampment. Wishing to attack when the camp was at its most vulnerable, the militiamen laid siege to those who remained behind. Many lives were lost in this skirmish, but Geronimo himself managed to escape.

At the very same time that this was going on, Cochise and Mangas Coloradas, Cochise's father-in-law, put together a sizeable contingent of Apache in preparations for a major showdown. This group headed for the settlement of Pinos Altos, New Mexico. The assault began during the early morning hours of September 27th, 1861. The Apache spread out and surrounded the town from all sides.

But the siege would be much more difficult than any of the Apache realized. The main trouble came from Confederate troops that were holed up in the town. The Apaches at this point had mostly dealt with Union soldiers, but as the Civil War heated up, some Confederates were beginning to spill over into this region as well. The Confederate troops in Pinos Altos ended up putting up a fierce fight, and most troubling for the Apaches was the use of their cannons.

As soon as the cannonballs began to fly, the Apaches were forced to give up their assault. These Confederate soldiers were under the leadership of Lieutenant Colonel John R. Baylor, who, after the battle, put together an additional unit of soldiers commanded by Captain Sherod Hunter. Union troops, meanwhile, were surging in from the west to take on this Confederate menace.

In order for these reinforcements to arrive, they had to go through Apache Pass. This set the stage for another confrontation between Cochise and the Americans in the summer of 1862. The conflict occurred when Cochise and his group, who were roaming the high parts of the pass, came across a band of some 140 Union troops camped down below. Cochise had nothing but vengeance on his mind this day, and without warning, he had his men open up on the troops below.

The Union soldiers were so unprepared for the assault that they immediately raised a white flag to sue for mercy. Seeing this sign of submission, Cochise ordered the Apache to hold their fire, and he traversed down to the encampment in order to speak with the leaders of the Union contingent. The Union officer proceeded to make nice with Cochise, giving him gifts of "tobacco and pemmican." This was the standard sort of bribe that was made for those wishing to make their way through Apache Pass. Initially, the Union officer thought that the appeasement had worked, but after Cochise departed, he found that while he was distracted with these overtures for peace, three of his men "had been shot, lanced, and stripped."

The Apaches, who had slipped into the camp to commit these atrocities, had already made their way back up to higher ground and were openly "mocking" the Union troops down below, as they were unable to do anything about it. Nevertheless, Cochise eventually allowed the troops to pass.

For the Apache, the most important aspect of the whole encounter was the intelligence that had been gathered. Cochise was able to rightfully estimate that this large influx of reinforcements meant that a great offensive was shaping up. Wishing to be prepared, he contacted Mangas Coloradas to forge an alliance. They were also able to join forces with Chief Victorio of the Warm Springs band, Chief Delgadito of the Copper Mines band, and the Apache warriors Juh and Nana. He also consulted Geronimo, who, while not a chief, was a strong leader and who was always more than ready to go on the warpath.

These plans would be disrupted in early January 1863 when Mangas Coloradas was double-crossed in a most terrible way. Mangas had tried to open up negotiations with US troops after sustaining an injury, but upon his approach, he was instead seized and made a prisoner of war. Mangas Coloradas was then brought to nearby Fort McLane, where he was placed under tight security.

Mangas Coloradas's security would be compromised, though, not from Apaches arriving to rescue him but rather from orders that came from within, as his security detail was openly encouraged by their commanding officer, American Brigadier General Joseph Rodman West, to mistreat Mangas. He told them, "Men, that old murderer has got away from every soldier command and has left a trail of blood for 500 miles on the old stage line. I want him dead or alive tomorrow morning. Do you understand? I want him dead."

Tipped off that their commanding officer would prefer the chief to be killed, his guards sought to actively agitate Magnas Coloradas. They wanted to provoke him enough so that he would lash out so they could say that they killed him in self-defense. And this is precisely what occurred on January 18th, 1863.

The chief, who was over six and a half foot tall, had been given a blanket that barely covered his body, and so, his feet kept finding their way out of the thin sheet he clung to. It was when the guards caught one of his feet sticking out that they decided to have a little "fun" with the chief by taking the tips of their bayonets, heating them up in the fire, and then burning the sleeping chief's exposed feet with the hot metal. Mangas attempted to ignore this indignity, but the guards wouldn't quit. And after he was poked with the hot bayonet several times, the chief got up and shouted, "I am no child to be played with!"

This obviously played right into his tormentors' hands, and they used his agitated stance as a reason to attack him. As soon as the chief got up, one of them shot him in the chest. Another soldier, hearing the commotion from outside, ran into the tent and finished Mangas off by shooting him right through the forehead. The indignities faced by Mangas Coloradas had sadly only just begun because after being given these mortal wounds, he was then scalped before being decapitated.

The grisly trophy of the chief's head was cooked over a fire, the flesh taken off, and the skull preserved. The skull was then sent off to a phrenologist in New York and was said to have been taken to the Smithsonian, although modern attempts to locate the skull have come up empty. When this event came to the knowledge of Geronimo, he was obviously enraged, to say the least. He would later refer to this episode as being, "Perhaps the greatest wrong ever done to the Indians."

With Mangas Coloradas gone, Geronimo had to consolidate his forces and head over to Apache Pass to consult with Cochise. As he watched and waited, he saw his first chance for retaliation on March 22nd, 1863. Through their various means of reconnaissance, the Apache had discovered an army installation underway in nearby Pinos Altos.

Geronimo led a raid that allowed the Apache to steal some sixty horses from the US troops. The US military was caught completely off-guard, and they were virtually unable to mount any kind of pursuit. Geronimo had become an expert at conducting lighting raids. This kind of hit-and-run guerrilla warfare was where he really excelled, but little did he know that he was about to bring the full fury of the US Army right down on top of him.

Chapter 6 – Geronimo the Renegade

While Geronimo began exacting vengeance on US troops through multiple raids, the Civil War was winding down. And by the war's end in 1865, the US was no longer distracted by the insurrection of the Confederacy and was therefore able to focus all of its attention on the Apache attacks in America's West. The end of the war also meant a fresh influx of settlers heading from the now peaceful East in order to try their luck in the Wild West.

In order to get a handle on all the raids the Apache leveled against the newcomers, the federal government commissioned a new army base smack dab in the middle of the notoriously treacherous Apache Pass. It was this strong, reinforced presence that led Chief Cochise to once again seek negotiations with the United States. These overtures led to a meeting between Cochise and US General Oliver Howard on October 20th, 1870.

It was from this meeting that a plan was crafted to allow Cochise and his Apache to peacefully lay down their arms in exchange for agreeing to be relocated to a specially prepared reservation in the Canada Alamosa region of New Mexico. According to the agreement, the tribe would be provided with regular foodstuffs and other supplies to help them settle the land. At first, the deal seemed decent enough, and Cochise was ready to sign off on it. But at the last minute, the US mediators altered the bargain and changed the location of the reservation to a much less attractive piece of real estate nestled in the dry desert sands of Mescalero, in southern New Mexico.

Cochise, not wanting to accept the degraded proposition, backed out of the deal. He came back to the bargaining table in 1872, however, to see if decent terms could still be met. Geronimo was in attendance at this meeting. The talks went better than either Cochise or Geronimo could have imagined, with the US allowing the Apache to remain as stewards of Apache Pass.

This put a big burden on Cochise's shoulders because it was up to him to ensure that all those traveling through his land were not harmed by any member of his tribe. In other words, he was now the designated peacekeeper who had to make sure that no further hostile actions erupted. Cochise was quite happy with the deal, but no matter how good the terms may have been, Geronimo maintained his stiff upper lip.

As one eyewitness to the signing of the treaty, a certain Lieutenant Sladen related, "His [Geronimo's] sensual, cruel, crafty face, as well as his dissatisfied manner had prejudiced me against him from the start." Nevertheless, the peace deal between the US and the Apache had been achieved. But the funny thing is, although this ended the Apache raids on Americans, Geronimo was more than happy to continue launching raids against the Mexicans! As Geronimo would later explain, he viewed the deal as being between the United States, meaning it had no bearing on any actions committed by Apache in northern Mexico. Cochise was against these activities, but Geronimo was able to act of his own accord, and he sent bands of Apache who were loyal to him south of the Rio Grande on a regular basis. In one of these raids, Geronimo and his men came back with a prisoner, a little boy from Mexico whom they had kidnapped.

Geronimo was holding the child in the hopes that he could get a hefty ransom from the family he had stolen him from. But before

Geronimo could attempt to trade the boy for precious goods, his deeds came to light, and authorities immediately demanded that he return the boy to his family. United States officials alerted Cochise as to what had occurred, and Cochise then placed pressure on Geronimo to take the child back to his rightful home.

Geronimo, forced to cave in to the demands, allowed the boy to be picked up by US officials, who then brought the young one back to his grateful parents in Mexico. Nevertheless, even with the boy's return, Geronimo continued to attack Mexicans. But after the American government was petitioned by Mexico to do something to stop these incursions, the Apache were finally told that enough was enough.

This caused Cochise to finally rein in Geronimo. However, after being told that the violent raids into Mexico from those situated at Apache Pass had to stop, Geronimo decided to take his business elsewhere. And taking whoever would come with him, he decided to leave Apache Pass altogether and strike out on his own.

Chapter 7 – Resigned to His Fate

Chief Cochise had tried his best to keep the peace, but with Geronimo and his band essentially becoming renegades, he had reached his limit of control. It was in the midst of all this duress that Cochise was found to have stomach cancer. The disease would only worsen, and he passed away on June 8th, 1874. Upon his passing, his son, Taza, would take up the mantle of his father. Geronimo, at this point, was on the run from Mexican militias but had reemerged among the Apache.

The death of Cochise certainly created a time of uncertainty. And soon, this uncertainty would become downright precarious. The trouble began innocuously enough when some local Apaches got drunk and, in their intoxicated state, decided they needed more liquor. It's not so much the fact that they wanted more alcohol that was the problem but the way that they went about getting it.

They raided a local ranch, stole their supply of whiskey, and killed the ranchers in the process. This one event managed to bring the full wrath of the American settler community down on the Apache. Under pressure from the public, in 1876, the federal government determined that the Apache would be moved farther away from American settlements in order to protect its citizens from future raids.

Geronimo and his band of Apache began raiding again by the end of the year, but this time he wasn't raiding in Mexico. Instead, he decided to tear a warpath through Arizona. This, of course, would make Geronimo the number one enemy of the United States. Geronimo and his followers had established an enclave along the borderlands between Arizona and New Mexico, and from there, they rode around, robbing and killing American settlers of the Southwest with impunity.

However, he wouldn't be able to get away with it forever, and soon a group of well-trained troops, aided by Native American scouting patrols, discovered Geronimo's camp. Geronimo was startled awake one fine morning in January of 1877 to find his base surrounded by US troops. Geronimo and his warriors sought cover, but the bullets were whizzing by on all sides.

Nevertheless, with a ferocious charge and guns blazing, Geronimo and his men managed to fight their way out. Geronimo and his people were now in desperate need of a safe haven. They found their place of refuge among the Apache of the nearby Ojo Caliente Reservation. This group of Apache, based out of Hot Springs, New Mexico, was under the guidance of Apache Chief Victorio.

Although Victorio had been warned against taking in the fugitive, he allowed Geronimo and his men to stay. Victorio remarked at the time, "These people are not bothering us." Nevertheless, it wouldn't be long before Geronimo's presence would indeed begin to bother Victorio and his Apache, as the US Army soon came calling.

On April 21ˢᵗ, 1877, a military contingent, led by an Indian affairs agent named John Clum, came looking for Geronimo. Geronimo faced the summons head-on, confronting Clum with several Apaches backing him up. Clum arrived with what appeared to be a small band of "Apache police," Apaches who had been conscripted to work as hired muscle for the department of Indian Affairs.

Geronimo thought he had nothing to fear when he saw the ragtag band standing before him. So, when Clum cautioned him, "No harm will come to you if you listen with good ears," Geronimo, only seeing a small, disorganized force, was downright haughty in his response. He shouted, "Speak with discretion, and no harm will come to you!"

Clum stood firm and declared his intention to take Geronimo back to the reservation in San Carlos so that he could answer for "breaking his promises of peace." Staring at Clum and the few officers standing around him, Geronimo couldn't believe what he was hearing. Incensed, he shouted back, "We are not going to San Carlos with you, and unless you are very careful, you and your Apache police will not go back to San Carlos either. Your bodies will stay here at Ojo Caliente to make feed for coyotes!"

However, Clum knew exactly what he was doing and who he was dealing with. Unbeknownst to Geronimo, he had already been surrounded by several Apache officers, who were hiding just out of sight in a commissary building. They were lying in wait for the cue to strike. That cue was Clum slightly tugging on the brim of his hat. And as soon as the hiding Apache police force saw this, they all jumped up and ran out of the commissary, with all of them training their guns on Geronimo.

If Geronimo or one of his associates so much as moved a muscle, Geronimo most certainly would have been killed. However, Geronimo hesitated and only considered using his gun. In the end, even Geronimo had to accept defeat, and he allowed Clum to take his weapon away from him. The two were then able to sit and have a somewhat civil conversation.

Still, when Clum alluded to the fact that Geronimo would be in chains when being transported as a prisoner, Geronimo found his sense of rage once again and brought out a dagger. One of the Apache police officers was able to snatch it out of his hand in time, and a defeated Geronimo was finally resigned to his fate.

Chapter 8 – The Revolving Door of the Reservation

It was on May 20th, 1877, that a shackled Geronimo was hauled off to a reservation in San Carlos, Arizona. He wasn't allowed to roam free on the reservation; instead, he was immediately placed inside the San Carlos jail. Geronimo would stay inside this prison cell for the next several weeks. It's interesting to note that although Geronimo was being held in this manner, no charges had been brought against him. He was essentially being kept under wraps as an enemy combatant until further notice.

That further notice came several weeks later when Geronimo was abruptly released from bondage and permitted to walk the reservation just like any other Apache. Clum, meanwhile, had taken a leave of absence in order to go back east and get married. But he didn't go alone; he took a "troupe of twenty-two" Apache with him, including Cochise's heir, Chief Taza.

He took his guests all the way to Washington, DC, where Clum gave them a tour of the nation's capital. However, these festivities were abruptly curtailed when Taza suddenly perished from pneumonia on September 26th, 1877. As soon as the Apache back home heard of the death of their chief, the leadership was immediately passed to Taza's brother, Naiche.

Chief Naiche did his best to step up to the plate, but he was much less experienced than his older brother Taza, and the void left by his passing was obvious. This was the confusing and conflicted state of affairs at the San Carlos Reservation that Geronimo became a part of. Even though Geronimo was never a chief, he was by far the most experienced Apache leader on the reservation. And it wasn't long before many of the Apache began looking to him for leadership.

This was actually encouraged by the US officials in charge of the reservation, as they saw Geronimo as a bulwark of stability that just might be able to keep the chaos at bay. But as much as Geronimo's handlers wanted him to keep the status quo on the reservation, it wasn't long before Geronimo himself would grow restless. This restlessness would become rather apparent on August 1st, 1878, when Geronimo hosted a so-called "tiswin drunk."

Tiswin was an alcoholic beverage the Apache typically brewed from corn, and they used the drink in all types of ceremonies. A tiswin drunk was a special social gathering in which everyone partook of a rather strong brew of tiswin. It is said that as the night wore on, a very drunk Geronimo got into a fight with one of his nephews and proceeded to humiliate him in front of the entire tribe.

It's not exactly clear what brought on this conflict, but the results would prove fatal since the scolded young man ended up taking his own life. Once he sobered up, Geronimo must have felt pretty bad about what had transpired, so bad that he abruptly gathered his family and took off. Riding clear off the reservation, he ended up back at his old stomping grounds of Janos, in northern Mexico.

Here, Geronimo met up with some fellow Apaches that he knew from previous expeditions. At the time, these particular Apaches were trying to negotiate with the Mexican government. The Mexicans had requested that the Apache move farther down the Rio Grande near the town of Ojinaga, but this was not at all palatable to this group of

Apache. As such, it wasn't long until this group of warriors began conducting fresh raids on local Mexicans.

After Geronimo's arrival on the scene, the first of these excursions occurred on September 26th, 1878. For it was on this day that the group participated in a raid just to the south of Casas Grandes, waylaying a convoy of unlucky Mexicans as they traveled through a region called "Chocolate Pass." Men, women, and children were indiscriminately slaughtered by these vengeful Apache. However, the raiding would not last for very long, ultimately coming to an end on November 12th, 1878.

On that day, one of the main contingents of Apache that Geronimo had partnered with became the victims of deceit. Mexican officials had lured them out of hiding so that they could talk, trade, and drink. After the Mexicans were sure that the Apaches were good and drunk, Mexican troops came in and "wiped out two-thirds of the group." While this was transpiring, another batch of Mexican troops managed to ambush Geronimo's camp in the region of Sonora.

Geronimo would later recall the scene. "I do not know how they were able to find our camp, but they were shooting at us before we knew they were near. We were in the timber. We kept behind rocks and trees until we came within ten yards of their line, then we stood up and both sides shot until all the Mexicans were killed. We lost twelve warriors in this battle."

According to Geronimo's account, his group barely managed to fight the Mexicans off. In such a weakened state, and with reinforcements most certainly on the way, Geronimo had no choice but to head back north to the borderlands, where he and his followers could hide in the wilderness. In the meantime, Geronimo and his men continued to launch sporadic raids from their new hiding places.

This period of banditry would begin to wind down in late November 1879 when representatives from the San Carlos Reservation tracked Geronimo down, not to fight but to offer him a lasting peace. After all of the bloodshed that had been wrought, it's safe to say that such tidings came as a surprise, and Geronimo probably would have viewed them with suspicion if it wasn't for the fact that men he trusted, such as "subchief Gordo," were among the representatives. This familiarity made the proposal at least seem believable. Nevertheless, it took several days of talks to convince Geronimo to accept the offer. Geronimo finally agreed, and on January 7th, 1880, he stepped right through, what for him was fast becoming, the revolving door of the San Carlos Reservation.

In many ways, it's rather incredible that Geronimo, a known renegade, was allowed to return to the San Carlos Reservation. No one's quite sure how many people Geronimo may have killed during his raids. On the subject, he himself once remarked, "I have killed many Mexicans; I do not know how many, for frequently I did not count them. Some of them were not worth counting."

So, by his own admission, Geronimo had killed countless people, yet he was allowed to waltz back into the reservation, no questions asked. As much as the reservation system has been criticized, it's rather amazing how lenient the US officials were with Geronimo. Unlike Mangas Coloradas, who had faced a far worse fate, it seems that when it came to Geronimo, those in charge were willing to let bygones be bygones.

Nevertheless, San Carlos was not at all to Geronimo's liking, and it wasn't long before he was considering making a break for it once again. As Geronimo later described it, "We were treated very badly by the agents here also, and that made us want to leave. We were given rations but not all that we should have had, not all that belonged to us." In the meantime, by the time 1881 rolled around, another event would create great upheaval on the reservation.

The discord centered around an Apache medicine man called Nocadelklinny, who many Apache hailed as a divine mystic. Nocadelklinny gained a large following, which soon turned into an all-out insurrection against US authority on the reservation. In order to quickly defuse the situation, US officials sought to have Nocadelklinny brought into custody.

It was due to these efforts that, on August 30th, 1881, "two troops of cavalry and a company of Indian scouts" converged onto the scene to apprehend Nocadelklinny. In the process of securing the medicine man, the Apache scouts suddenly mutinied and joined up with Nocadelklinny's forces. This led to a pitched battle in which Nocadelklinny was killed. In the aftermath, many of Nocadelklinny's followers actually joined up with Geronimo.

For his part, Geronimo welcomed these disaffected warriors, but at the same time, he also realized that he would soon have the full force of the American government on his heels. Knowing that he couldn't remain where he was, Geronimo led the group off the reservation and back to the Mexican borderlands, which had provided refuge to him for much of his life.

Since Geronimo holed up in the Sierra Madre Mountains, just south of the border, the US soldiers were initially unable to follow. This was due to Mexican laws that, quite naturally, prohibited US troop movement across the Mexican border. But due to an agreement forged in the summer of 1882, called the "hot pursuit agreement," US soldiers were eventually given special permission to cross the border if they were pursuing Apaches.

After several engagements, Geronimo and his followers finally set up camp in Casas Grandes. Here, rather than raiding, Geronimo and his company actually began to engage in trading. But the item that was most often bartered would prove to be the Apaches' undoing. They would go into town to retrieve a particularly strong brew of alcohol called mezcal. Geronimo would later recall, "We began to trade, and the Mexicans gave us mescal [mezcal]. Soon nearly all the Indians were drunk. While they were drunk, two companies of Mexican troops, from another town attacked us, killed twenty Indians, and captured many more. We fled in all directions."

It was shortly after this episode that US General George Crook was able to intercept Geronimo and what was left of his followers. Knowing that he was beaten, Geronimo entered into negotiations with General Crook. In the end, Geronimo was once again compelled to make his return to the San Carlos Reservation. Geronimo and his band agreed to go back to the reservation, and as before, all seemed to be forgiven.

Chapter 9 – Retired from the Range

During his first few years back at San Carlos, Geronimo tried to live by the rules of the reservation and become a peaceful resident. He even tried his luck as a farmer, planting what he could in the arid soil of the reservation. But no matter how hard he tried to adapt, Geronimo could not get used to the sedentary life of living in one spot. And he soon began to consider going off the reservation once again.

The whole reservation had been growing increasingly restless in the meantime over the rules and regulations they were being made to follow. Particularly distressing to the Apache was the fact that they had been forbidden their occasional "tiswin drunk," in which they consumed large amounts of alcohol, and they were also told not to beat their wives. All of this sounds completely absurd by modern standards, but excessive drinking and being able to "punish" their wives with physical violence were a part of Apache culture at the time. And the mere fact that outsiders would attempt to tell them how to live their lives was met with great animosity. In May of 1885, the Apache held a kind of protest by holding a massive "tiswin drunk" ceremony. Geronimo was, of course, one of the main rabble-rousers during the whole ordeal.

The next day, Geronimo and his allies went to the camp of a certain Lieutenant Britton Davis to air their grievances. Geronimo and several others were said to have been visibly intoxicated at the time. The soberest among them was a chief by the name of Loco, who served as the main mouthpiece of the group. Davis tried to tell the Apache that it was for their own good that certain changes to their customs were being made.

One of the tribal elders, an Apache called Nana, took umbrage to Davis's words, shouting to an interpreter, "Tell the Nantan Enchau [Nantan Enchau was a nickname given to Davis which, roughly translated, meant "stout chief"] that he can't advise me how to treat my women. He is only a boy. I killed men before he was born."

Shortly thereafter, another Apache named Chihuahua, who disagreed with the prohibition on alcohol, openly challenged Davis, proclaiming, "We all drank tiswin last night, all of us in the tent and outside. What are you going to do about it? Are you going to put us all in jail? You have no jail big enough even if you could put us all in jail."

Lieutenant Davis must have realized that the frustrated Apache had a point. The US Army was attempting to curtail the behavior of the Apache, but they didn't have enough resources on the reservation to enforce the arbitrary rules that they had set. Geronimo, taking note of this impotence, was now ready to make another break for it. And on May 17th, he gathered together some 144 Apache and left the reservation.

Geronimo led his entourage to his old stomping grounds of the Sierra Madre Mountains in northern Mexico. Here, Geronimo once again led lighting raids against local settlements and passersby while always staying one step ahead of his pursuers. On August 7th, however, Geronimo was nearly captured when a group of Apache scouts was sent into the region to look for him.

Geronimo's encampment was caught off guard, and Geronimo found himself under heavy fire and was forced to flee. What was left of his followers then regrouped and joined back up with Geronimo. He and his men would then go on an odyssey, traveling throughout several regions in northern Mexico and the southeastern United States. By September, some 5,000 US troops were in hot pursuit. However, Geronimo managed to masterfully elude his pursuers, crisscrossing into Arizona and then back into northern Mexico.

But by 1886, Geronimo was just about out of gas, and he began moving toward negotiations with US officials once more. In March of that year, Geronimo began to meet with General George Crook to discuss terms. This event was actually documented by a photographer who was in attendance, giving us one of the few early glimpses of what Geronimo was like in the flesh.

Geronimo often appeared angry in these early photos, and during this particular exchange, he most certainly was. He had just been informed by Crook that he would accept nothing but his "unconditional surrender." And if Geronimo did not surrender according to these terms, he and his band would be hunted down to the last man. At first, Geronimo seemed like he was going to cave to the pressure and surrender, but by March 31st, he got his second wind, and after gathering a core group of people around him, he snuck off early in the morning before Crook would even realize he was gone.

Crook, who was very wary of dealing with Geronimo, would ultimately be replaced by General Nelson Miles on April 11th, 1886. It would be General Miles who would put an end to Geronimo's freedom once and for all, but not before Geronimo and his men led a reign of terror all over the Southwest. One of the most appalling of these episodes—and the most well documented—occurred on April 27th, 1886.

For it was on this day that Geronimo raided an Arizona ranch near the Santa Cruz River, leaving a traumatic memory on the rancher that would scar him for life. The man's name was Artisan Peck, and he was busy herding his cattle when Geronimo and his warriors descended upon his homestead. They confronted and killed the man's wife, as well as his infant child, before taking Artisan's ten-year-old niece as a prisoner. They then went outside and ambushed Peck. Artisan Peck was badly beaten and was even stripped naked. For reasons only known to Geronimo, he allowed Peck to live. Beaten, bloody, robbed of everything—even the shirt on his back—Peck wandered back home where he was greeted by the grisly sight of his slain wife and child. Peck would later testify that it was indeed Geronimo who led the rampage on his home.

Geronimo would first enter into talks with General Miles in late August through his lieutenant, a man named Charles Gatewood. Even though Miles wasn't present for this first meeting, Geronimo was sure to pump Gatewood with plenty of questions in regard to General Crook's successor. This preliminary meeting with Gatewood would then produce another meeting in which Geronimo would meet with General Miles directly.

These efforts would bear fruit in the form of Geronimo's surrender on September 4th. Public sentiment in Arizona against Geronimo, in the meantime, was so bad that Miles knew that he had to quickly remove Geronimo from the region. Since Geronimo had admittedly killed so many people during his forays, it's pretty understandable that the loved ones of those who were slain might want to see him tried in a court of law.

But instead of being presented in a courtroom in Arizona, he was quietly shipped off to Fort Sam Houston in San Antonio, Texas. Here, he was held as a prisoner of war for several weeks before being relocated to Pensacola, Florida. Despite past depredations, General Miles had promised Geronimo that the "slate had been wiped clean." Geronimo and his warriors arrived in Pensacola at Fort Pickens on October 25th, 1886.

By then, Geronimo's fame had preceded him, and as soon as his train arrived at the station, huge multitudes of curious onlookers wishing to get a glimpse of the notorious renegades. Once Geronimo and his fifteen fellow Apache were ushered past the crowds, they were brought to what would be their temporary home at the fort.

They were divided up between two rooms that had wooden bunks available for each man to sleep on. They were also given new clothes to wear: military-styled "brown canvas suits," along with army boots, socks, and underclothing. For food, they were given regular rations, and while at the fort, they were made to earn their keep by clearing brush out of the courtyard a few hours a day.

Geronimo would stay at Fort Pickens until he was transferred to Mount Vernon Barracks in Alabama in May of 1888. Here, Geronimo was reunited with many of the other Apache he had been separated from since his last "breakout" from the reservation. Many were happy to see him, but others seemed to harbor a grudge against him, blaming him for their current plight.

Geronimo was given his own "two-room log cabin" right in the middle of the camp. This position seemed to signify that Geronimo was an Apache of importance, whether all of the other Apache agreed to this distinction or not. Geronimo, along with his people, were put to a wide variety of tasks to keep themselves busy. At one point, Geronimo was even taught how to write his name and make "walking sticks."

Already a celebrity, the old Apache warrior would then spend time making wooden walking sticks with his name carved into them as a kind of autograph. He sold these for a dollar a piece to the enthusiastic "tourists" who came by the community. Geronimo would stay in Alabama until 1894, when he was moved to what would be his final place of residence, Fort Sill, Oklahoma.

Geronimo was well respected at this fort for his obedience and hard work in whatever task was requested of him. His only real trouble came in 1898 due to a gross misunderstanding of someone who had tattled on him. The Spanish-American War had just kicked off over in Cuba, and many Apache had enlisted, but Geronimo, who was by then well into his seventies, was, of course, considered too old to fight.

One evening, a young woman overheard Geronimo joking with some friends about how easy it would be to "make a break for it" with everyone off fighting the war. These few idle words set off the rumor that Geronimo was planning on leading a new revolt.

Taking the matter quite seriously, the US officials in charge brought Geronimo in for questioning. Geronimo immediately denied that he had any such intentions and expressed shock and indignation that anyone suspected him of plotting such a thing. Nevertheless, he was placed under close watch for the next few weeks until the fears and suspicions died down.

After this episode, Geronimo would live out the rest of his days in relative peace. At times, he was even allowed to leave the reservation for special occasions, such as when he took part in special events highlighting Native American culture. Geronimo also participated in the so-called Wild West Shows, which were very popular at the time. They were the brainchild of William F. Cody, better known as Buffalo Bill.

Here, in these theatrical renditions of what life was like in the West, it must have been with some sad irony that Geronimo acted out what it was like to be a free Apache riding the range, as he was still considered a prisoner of the US government. But Geronimo was a celebrity all the same, and his fame would lead him to even take part in the 1904 World's Fair. Perhaps the most spectacular event that Geronimo would take part in, though, was when he participated in the inaugural procession of Teddy Roosevelt in 1905. Geronimo, flanked by various Native American chieftains, proudly rode out before the crowds. It was a much humbler Geronimo who had an audience with the new president after the parade was over. With tears in his eyes, Geronimo asked Teddy to "take the ropes from the hands" of the Native Americans. "The ropes have been on my hands for many years and we want to go back to our home in Arizona."

To this emotional display, Teddy answered bluntly, "When you lived in Arizona you had a bad heart and killed many of my people. I cannot grant the request you make for yet a while. We will have to wait and see how you act." And wait and see they did, with nothing coming from the conversation, at least in regards to Geronimo, for his life would ultimately come to a close in the spring of 1909.

He was riding on a horse at the reservation when he fell and injured himself. The accident occurred in a fairly isolated spot, and it took some time for anyone to find him. Being exposed to the cold for so long did not bode well for Geronimo, and it led to him passing away of pneumonia on February 17th, 1909.

Conclusion

Geronimo was a man who survived by his wits. He faced much hardship in his life, but he was able to navigate hurdles that most would find impossible. Who else could live on the run from both the United States and Mexican armies, passing back and forth from one wilderness to the other, but Geronimo?

And who else, when cornered and captured by their enemies, would have the charisma to convince them to not only spare his life but aid in rehabilitating his image? Once Geronimo had retired from the warpath, he became a kind of folk hero and celebrity, and he represented the best of Americana.

Geronimo, however, wasn't just the caricature of the Wild West that later Americans created. He was a living, breathing man with a proud Apache background. Geronimo and his Apache followers were, in many ways, the last stand against Western expansion. The Apache were known to be fierce warriors—and Geronimo was among the fiercest—so it should be no surprise that he oversaw some of the last great uprisings against the growing hegemony of the United States government. His incredible resistance would be admired by friend and foe alike.

And he has remained a symbol of endurance and tenacity for the American military long after his death. After all, no paratrooper jump would be the same without someone shouting, "Geronimo!" Osama Bin Laden, the former leader of Al Qaeda, was also codenamed Geronimo due to his stubborn resistance to be captured. Whether you love him or hate him, Geronimo's name is one that continues to reverberate in the American psyche to this very day.

Appendix A: Further Reading and Reference

Geronimo. Robert M. Utley. Yale University Press, 2012.
Geronimo: My Life. Geronimo & S. M. Barrett (editor). Dover Publications, 1906.

Here's another book by Captivating History
that you might be interested in

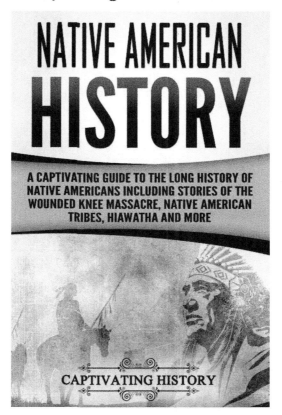

Printed in Great Britain
by Amazon

54080220R00030